Hits

contents

COVER PHOTO BY KAREN MILLER
INSIDE PHOTOS BY BRAD STANLEY
LOGO DESIGN BY TOM NIKOSEY

Bob & Cole Seger

ROLL ME AWAY
WORDS AND MUSIC BY BOB SEGER

This song always started out full throttle but one time between takes piano player Roy Bittan and drummer Russ Kunkel began playing the intro in a far more subtle and subdued manner. Everyone then followed and fell in, including me, singing live. Ordinarily, we never have the tape machine recording between takes but producer Jimmy Lovine and engineer Shelly Yakus had astutely left it on. When we listened back, we loved it and it quickly became the final version.

Took a look down a westbound road, right away
I made my choice
Headed out to my big two-wheeler, I was tired of my
    own voice
Took a bead on the northern plains and just rolled
    that power on

Twelve hours out of Mackinaw City stopped in a bar
    to have a brew
Met a girl and we had a few drinks and I told her
    what I'd decided to do
She looked out the window a long long moment then
    she looked into my eyes
She didn't have to say a thing, I knew what she was
    thinkin'

Roll, roll me away, won't you roll me away tonight
I too am lost, I feel double-crossed and I'm sick of
    what's wrong and what's right
We never even said a word, we just walked out
and got on that bike
And we rolled
And we rolled clean out of sight

We rolled across the high plains
Deep into the mountains
Felt so good to me
Finally feelin' free

Somewhere along a high road
The air began to to run cold
She said she missed her home
I headed on alone

Stood alone on a mountain top, starin' out at the
    Great Divide
I could go east, I could go west, it was all up to
me to decide
Just then I saw a young hawk flyin' and my soul
    began to rise
And pretty soon
My heart was singin'

Roll, roll me away, I'm gonna roll me away tonight
Gotta keep rollin', gotta keep ridin', keep searchin'
till find I what's right
And as the sunset faded I spoke to the faintest
first starlight
And I said next time
Next Time
We'll get it right

NIGHT MOVES
WORDS AND MUSIC BY BOB SEGER

It was 2:00 am and our guitar player Drew Abbott and sax player Alto Reed had already left the studio for the drive back to Detroit. With bass player Chris Campbell, drummer Charlie Martin and me, playing acoustic guitar, we recorded it. I think we did five takes. The next day we added a local guitar player and piano player and then some female singers from Montréal who happened to be in town. When people ask "Do you know when you've written a hit?" the usual answer is no. This song was an exception.

I was little too tall
Could've used a few pounds
Tight pants points hardly reknown
She was a black-haired beauty with big dark eyes
And points all her own sitting way up high
Way up firm and high

Out past the cornfields where the woods got heavy
Out in the back seat of my '60 Chevy
Workin' on mysteries without any clues
Workin' on our night moves
Tryin' to make some front page drive-in news
Workin' on our night moves
In the summertime
In the sweet summertime

We weren't in love, oh no, far from it
We weren't searchin' for some pie in the sky 'summit
We were just young and restless and bored
Livin' by the sword
And we'd steal away every chance we could
To the backroom, to the alley or the trusty woods
I used her, she used me
But neither one cared
We were gettin' our share

Workin' on our night moves
Tryin' to lose the awkward teenage blues
Workin' on our night moves
And it was summertime

And oh the wonder
We felt the lightning
And we waited on the thunder
Waited on the thunder

I awoke last night to the sound of thunder
How far off I sat and wondered
Started humming a song from 1962
Ain't it funny how the night moves
When you just don't seem to have as much to lose
Strange how the night moves
With autumn closing in

TURN THE PAGE

WORDS AND MUSIC BY BOB SEGER

Our first headline shows ever in a large (twelve thousand seat) hall were the two shows at Cobo Arena, September 4th and 5th, 1975. I remember while I was singing this how nice it was to have such good on-stage monitors. I had never heard my voice so well while performing.

On a long and lonesome highway east of Omaha
You can listen to the engine moanin' out his one note song
You can think about the woman or the girl you knew
   the night before
But your thoughts will soon be wandering the way
   they always do
When you're ridin' sixteen hours and there's nothin'
   much to do
And you don't feel much like ridin', you just wish the
   trip was through

Here I Am
on the road again
There I am
Up on the stage
Here I go
Playin' star again
There I go
Turn the page

Well you walk into a restaurant, strung out from the road
And you feel the eyes upon you as you're shakin' off the cold
You pretend it doesn't bother you but you just want
   to explode
Most times you can't hear 'em talk, other time you can
All the same old clichés, "is that a woman or a man?"
And you always seem outnumbered, you don't dare
   make a stand

Here I am
on the road again
There I am
Up on the stage
Here I go
Playin' star again
There I go
Turn the page

Out there in the spotlight you're a million miles away
Every ounce of energy you try to give away
As the sweat pours out your body like the music that
   you play
Later in the evening as you lie awake in bed
With the echoes from the amplifiers ringin' in your head
You smoke the day's last cigarette, rememberin' what she said

Here I am
on the road again
There I am
Up on the stage
Here I go
Playin' star again
There I go
Turn the page

Here I am
on the road again
There I am
Up on the stage
Here I go
Playin' star again
There I go
there I go

YOU'LL ACCOMP'NY ME

WORDS AND MUSIC BY BOB SEGER

This again was one of those rare times when our bass player Chris, our drummer David Teegarden, and I were alone in the studio. Like "Night Moves," I played acoustic guitar and much later we added Bill Payne on keyboards and the female background singers.

A gypsy wind is blowing warm tonight
The sky is starlit and the time is right
And still you're tellin' me you have to go
Before you leave there's something you should know
Yeah something you should know babe

I've seen you smiling in the summer sun
I've seen your long hair flying when you run
I've made my mind up that it's meant to be
Someday lady you'll accomp'ny me

Someday lady you'll accomp'ny me
Out where the rivers meet the sounding sea
You're high above me now, you're wild and free ah but
Someday lady you'll accomp'ny me
Someday lady you'll accomp'ny me

Some people say that love's a losin' game
You start with fire but you lose the flame
The ashes smolder but the warmth's soon gone
You end up cold and lonely on your own

I'll take my chances babe I'll risk it all
I'll win you love or I'll take the fall
I've made my mind up girl it's meant to be
Someday lady you'll accomp'ny me
Someday lady you'll accomp'ny me
It's written down somewhere, it's got to be
You're high above me flyin' wild and free
Oh but someday lady you'll accomp'ny me
Someday lady you'll accomp'ny me

Someday lady you'll accomp'ny me
Out where the rivers meet the sounding sea
I feel it in my soul, It's meant to be
Oh someday lady you'll accomp'ny me
Someday lady you'll accomp'ny me

HOLLYWOOD NIGHTS
WORDS AND MUSIC BY BOB SEGER

The chorus to this song came into my head one night in 1977 as I was driving through the Hollywood Hills. Our drummer, David Teegarden, played an entire set of drums as we recorded and overdubbed another entire set of drums playing a different pattern. In other words, there's two sets of everything: snare, kick drum, hi-hat, etc. Billy Payne (of Little Feat) sat in with us for the first time and played the last two instruments, piano and organ. When he was done, he asked for a tape to listen to on the way home. He called me the next day and said while he'd been listening, he looked down and found himself going 100 miles an hour on the freeway.

She stood there bright as the sun on the California
   coast
He was a midwestern boy on his own
She looked at him with those soft eyes, so innocent
   and blue
He knew right then he was too far from home
He was too far from home

She took his hand and she led him along that golden
   beach
They watched the waves tumble over the sand
They drove for miles and miles up those twisting
   turning roads
Higher and higher and higher they climbed

And those Hollywood nights
In those Hollywood hills
She was looking so right
In her diamonds and frills
All those big city nights
In those high rolling hills
Above all the lights
She had all of the skills

He'd headed west 'cause he felt that a change would do him good
See some old friends, good for the soul
She had been born with a face that would let her get her way
He saw that face and he lost all control
He had lost all control

Night after night, day after day, it went on and on
Then came that morning he woke up alone
He spent all night staring down at the lights of LA
Wondering if he could ever go home

And those Hollywood nights
In those Hollywood hills
It was looking so right
It was giving him chills
In those big city nights
In those high rolling hills
Above all the lights
With a passion that kills

In those Hollywood nights
In those Hollywood hills
She was looking so right
In her diamonds and frills
All those big city nights
In those high rolling hills
Above all the lights
She had all of the skills

STILL THE SAME
WORDS AND MUSIC BY BOB SEGER

It was Chris Campbell, David Teegarden, and me in the studio when we cut this. People have asked me for years who it's about. It's an amalgamation of characters I met when I first went to Hollywood. All "Type A" personalities: oveachieving, driven.

You always won, everytime you placed a bet
You're still damn good, no one's gotten you yet
Everytime they were sure they had you caught
You were quicker than they thought
You'd just turn your back and walk.

You always said, the cards would never do you
   wrong
The trick you said was never play the game too long
A gambler's share, the only risk that you would take
The only loss you could forsake
The only bluff you couldn't fake

And you're still the same
I caught up with you yesterday
Moving game to game
No one standing in your way
Turning on the charm
Long enough to get you by
You're still the same
You still aim high

There you stood, everybody watched you play
I just turned and walked away
I had nothing left to say
'Cause you're still the same
You're still the same
Moving game to game
Some things never change
You're still the same

OLD TIME ROCK & ROLL

WORDS AND MUSIC BY GEORGE JACKSON
AND THOMAS E. JONES III

*This track was sent to me by the Muscle Shoals
Rhythm Section from Alabama as a demo with
a different singer. I rewrote the verses but asked
for no writing credit (I wish I had). Next to
Patsy Cline's "Crazy", it's the most popular
jukebox single of all time.*

Just take those old records off the shelf
I'll sit and listen to 'em by myself
Today's music ain't got the same soul
I like that old time rock 'n' roll
Don't try to take me to a disco
You'll never even get me out on the floor
In ten minutes I'll be late for the door
I like that old time rock 'n' roll

Still like that old time rock 'n' roll
That kind of music just soothes the soul
I reminisce about the days of old
With that old time rock 'n' roll

Won't go to hear them play a tango
I'd rather hear some blues or funky old soul
There's only one sure way to get me to go
Start playing old time rock 'n' roll
Call me relic, call me what you will
Say I'm old-fashioned, say I'm over the hill
Today's music ain't got the same soul
I like that old time rock 'n' roll

Still like that old time rock 'n' roll
That kind of music just soothes the soul
I reminisce about the days of old
With that old time rock 'n' roll

WE'VE GOT TONIGHT

WORDS AND MUSIC BY BOB SEGER

*The original title of the song was "This Old
House" and it was about rock and roll music. I
loved the chords and rewrote the lyric after I
saw Robert Redford in The Sting say to a
waitress, "It's four in the morning and I don't
know nobody."*

I know it's late, I know you're weary
I know your plans don't include me
Still here we are, both of us lonely
Longing for shelter from all that we see
Why should we worry, no one will care girl
Look at the stars so far away
We've got tonight, who needs tomorrow?
We've got tonight babe
Why don't you stay?

Deep in my soul, I've been so lonely
All of my hopes, fading away
I've longed for love, like everyone else does
I know I'll keep searching, even after today
So there it is girl, I've said it all now

And here we are babe, what do you say?
We've got tonight, who needs tomorrow?
We've got tonight, babe
Why don't you stay?

I know it's late, I know you're weary
I know your plans don't include me
Still here we are, both of us lonely
Both of us lonely

We've got tonight, who needs tomorrow?
Let's make it last, let's find a way
Turn out the lights, come take my hand now
We've got tonight babe
Why don't you stay?
Why don't you stay?

Matthew & Craig Frost

AGAINST THE WIND

WORDS AND MUSIC BY BOB SEGER

*My old friend, Glen Frey of the Eagles, had an
idea that our guitarist Drew Abbott should play
along with the piano solo. He and I then went
out and did the background vocals together. The
line "Wish I didn't know now what I didn't know
then" bothered me for the longest time but
everyone I knew loved it so I left it in. It has
since appeared in several hits by other artists,
so I guess it's O.K.*

It seems like yesterday
But it was long ago
Janey was lovely, she was the queen of my nights
There in the darkness with the radio playing low
And the secrets that we shared
The mountains that we moved
Caught like a wildfire out of control
Till there was nothing left to burn and nothing left to prove
And I remember what she said to me
How she swore that it never would end
I remember how she held me oh so tight
Wish I didn't know now what I didn't know then

Against the wind
We were runnin' against the wind
We were young and strong, we were runnin'
against the wind

And the years rolled slowly past
And I found myself alone
Surrounded by strangers I thought were my friends
I found myself further and further from my home
And I guess I lost my way
There were oh so many roads
I was living to run and running to live
Never worried about paying or even how much I owed
Moving eight miles a minute for months at a time
Breaking all of the rules that would bend
I began to find myself searching
Searching for shelter again and again

Chris & Alexandra Campbell

Against the wind
A little something against the wind
I found myself seeking shelter against the wind

Well those drifters days are past me now
I've got so much more to think about
Deadlines and commitments
What to leave in, what to leave out

Against the wind
I'm still runnin' against the wind
I'm older now but still runnin' against the wind
Well I'm older now and still runnin'
Against the wind

MAINSTREET
WORDS AND MUSIC BY BOB SEGER

*Many people have asked me what street I'm
talking about in this song. It's actually Ann
Street, just off Main Street in Ann Arbor,
Michigan, where I grew up and went to school.
There was a pool hall (I can't remember the
name) where they had girls dancing in the window and R&B bands playing on the weekends.*

I remember standing on the corner at midnight
Trying to get my courage up
There was this long lovely dancer in a little
    club downtown
I loved to watch her do her stuff
Through the long lonely nights she filled my sleep
Her body softly swaying to that smoky beat
Down on Mainstreet

In the pool halls, the hustlers and the losers
I used to watch 'em through the glass
Well I'd stand outside at closing time
Just to watch her walk on past
Unlike all the other ladies she looked so
    young and sweet
As she made her way alone down that empty street
Down on Mainstreet

And sometimes even now, when I'm feeling lonely
    and beat
I drift back in time and I find my feet
Down on Mainstreet
Down on Mainstreet

THE FIRE INSIDE
WORDS AND MUSIC BY BOB SEGER

*I rewrote this song so many times, I can't
remember the original lyric. Oddly, for me, I
kept rewriting the first verse. I've never done
that before or since.*

There's a hard moon risin' on the streets tonight
There's a reckless feeling in your heart as you head
    out tonight
Through the concrete canyons to the midtown lights
Where the lastest neon promises are burning bright

Past the open windows on the darker streets
Where unseen angry voices flash and children cry
Past the phony posers with their worn out lines
The tired new money dressed to the nines
The low life dealers with their bad designs
And the dilettantes with their open minds

You're out on the town, safe in the crowd
Ready to go for the ride
Searching the eyes, looking for clues
There's no way you can hide
The fire inside

Well you've been to the clubs and the discotheques
Where they deal one another from the bottom of a
    deck of promises
Where the cautious loners and emotional wrecks
Do an acting stretch as a way to hide the obvious
And the lights go down and they dance real close
And for one brief instant they pretend they're safe
    and warm

Then the beat gets louder and the mood is gone
The darkness scatters as the lights flash on
They hold one another just a little too long
And they move apart and then move on

On to the street, on to the next
Safe in the knowledge that they tried
Faking the smile, hiding the pain
Never satisfied
The fire inside
Fire inside

Now the hour is late and he thinks you're asleep
You listen to him dress and you listen to him leave
    like you knew he would
You hear his car pull away in the street
Then you move to the door and you lock it when
    he's gone for good

Then you walk to the window and stare at the moon
Riding high and lonesome through a starlit sky
And it comes to you how all slips away
Youth and beauty are gone one day
No matter what you dream or feel or say
It ends in dust and disarray

Like wind on the plains, sand through the glass
Waves rolling in with the tide
Dreams die hard and we watch them erode
But we cannot be denied
The fire inside

LIKE A ROCK
WORDS AND MUSIC BY BOB SEGER

My fondest memory of this recording is of David Cole and me listening to Rick Vito play the slide guitar solo late one night at Rumbo Studios in LA. It was the single most spectacular overdub I'd ever heard.

Stood there boldly
Sweatin' in the sun
Felt like a million
Felt like number one
The height of summer
I'd never felt that strong
Like a rock

I was eighteen
Didn't have a care
Working for peanuts
Not a dime to spare
But I was lean and
Solid everywhere
Like a rock

My hands were steady
My eyes were clear and bright
My walk had purpose
My steps were quick and light
And I held firmly
To what I felt was right
Like a rock

Like a rock, I was strong as I could be
Like a rock, nothin' ever got to me
Like a rock, I was something to see
Like a rock

And I stood arrow straight
Unecumbered by the weight
Of all these hustlers and the their schemes
I stood proud, I stood tall
High above it all
I still believed in my dreams

Twenty years now
Where'd they go?
Twenty years
I don't know
I sit and I wonder sometimes
Where they've gone

And sometimes late at night
When I'm bathed in the firelight
The moon comes callin' a ghostly white
And I recall
I recall

Like a rock, standin' arrow straight
Like a rock, chargin' from the gate
Like a rock, carryin' the weight
Like a rock

Like a rock, the sun upon my skin
Like a rock, hard against the wind
Like a rock, I see myself again
Like a rock

C'EST LA VIE
WORDS AND MUSIC BY CHUCK BERRY

We had a lot of fun doing this old Chuck Berry nugget. Entirely live. No overdubs.

It was a teenage wedding and the old folks
   wished 'em well
You could see that Pierre did truly love the mademoiselle
And now the young monsieur and madam have rung
   the chapel bell
C'est la vie say the old folks, it goes to show you
   never can tell

They finished off an apartment with a two-room
   Roebuck sale
The coolerator was jammed with TV dinners and
   ginger ale
And when Pierre found work, the little money comin'
   worked out well
C'est la vie say the old folks, it goes to show you
   never can tell

They had a hi-fi phono, boy did they let it blast
Seven hundred little records, all blues, rock rhythm
   and jazz
But when the sun went down, the volume went down
   as well
C'est la vie say the old folks, it goes to show you
   never can tell

They bought a souped-up jitney, it was a
   cherry red '53
And drove it down to New Orleans to celebrate
   their anniversary
It was there where Pierre was wedded to the lovely
   mademoiselle
C'est la vie say the old folks, it goes to show you
   never can tell

They had a teenage wedding and the old folks
   wished 'em well
You could see that Pierre did truly love the mademoiselle
And now the young monsieur and madam have rung
   the chapel bell
C'est la vie say the old folks, it goes to show you
   never can tell

*Chelsea, Alto &
Victoria Reed*

IN YOUR TIME

WORDS AND MUSIC BY BOB SEGER

A new song written for my son Cole.

In your time
The innocence will fall away
In your time
The mission bells will toll
All along
The corridors and river beds
There'll be sign
In your time

Towering waves
Will crash across your southern capes
Massive storms
Will reach your eastern shores
Fields of green
Will tumble through your summer days
by design
In your time

Feel the wind
And set yourself the bolder course
Keep your heart
As open as a shrine
You'll sail the perfect line

And after all
The dead ends and the lessons learned
After all
The stars have turned to stone
There'll be peace
Across the great unbroken void
All benign
In your time
You'll be fine
In your time

ROLL ME AWAY

Words and Music by
BOB SEGER

And we rolled, _ and we rolled _ clean out of

sight.

We rolled _ a - cross the high plains _ deep _ in - to the
Some - where _ a - long a high road _ the air _ be - gan to

D.S. al Coda

NIGHT MOVES

Words and Music by
BOB SEGER

And we'd steal a - way ev - 'ry chance we could,

to the back room, to the al - ley, or the trust - y woods. _____

I used her, she used me, ___ but nei - ther one cared. _____

We were get - tin' our share, ___ work - in' on our

Strange how the night moves, ___ with au-tumn clos-ing in. ___

Tempo I

Night moves.
Lead vocal ad lib.

1-7

Night moves.

8

Vocal ad lib. continues

TURN THE PAGE

Words and Music by
BOB SEGER

28

D.S. al Coda

2. Well, you ___ Here I

CODA

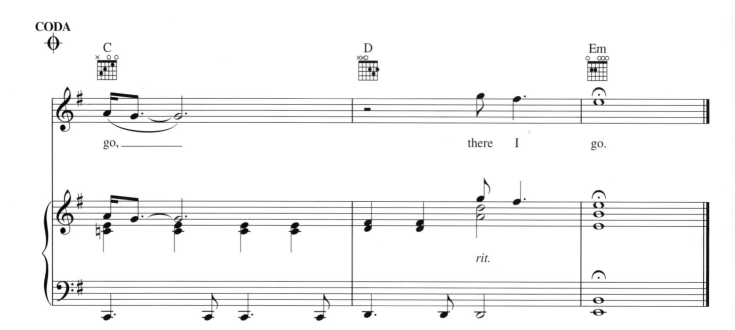

go, ___ there I go.

rit.

Additional Lyrics

2. Well, you walk into a restaurant strung out from the road
   And you feel the eyes upon you as you're shakin' off the cold;
   You pretend it doesn't bother you but you just want to explode.
   Most times you can't hear 'em talk, other times you can,
   All the same old cliches, "Is that a woman or a man?"
   And you always seem out numbered, you don't dare make a stand.

3. Out there in the spotlight you're a million miles away.
   Every ounce of energy you try to give away
   As the sweat pours out your body like the music that you play.
   Later in the evening as you lie awake in bed
   With the echos of the amplifiers ringing in your head,
   You smoke the day's last cigarette remembering what she said.

YOU'LL ACCOMP'NY ME

Words and Music by
BOB SEGER

HOLLYWOOD NIGHTS

Words and Music by
BOB SEGER

She took his hand and she led him a - long that gold - en beach.
Night af - ter night and day af - ter day it went on and on.

They watched the waves tum - ble o - ver the sand.
Then came that morn - ing he woke up a - lone.

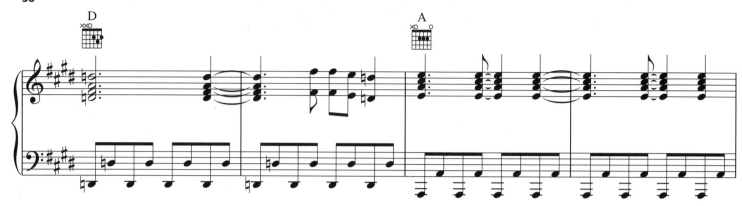

D.S. al Coda

CODA

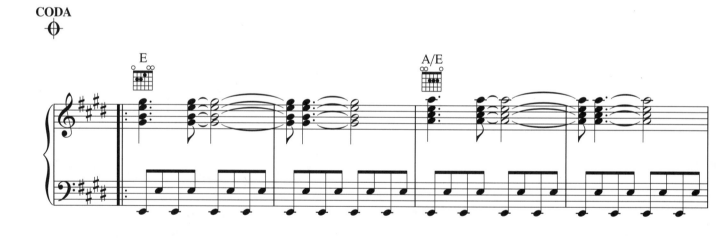

Repeat and Fade

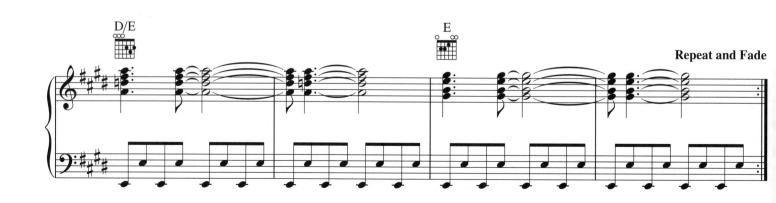

STILL THE SAME

Words and Music by
BOB SEGER

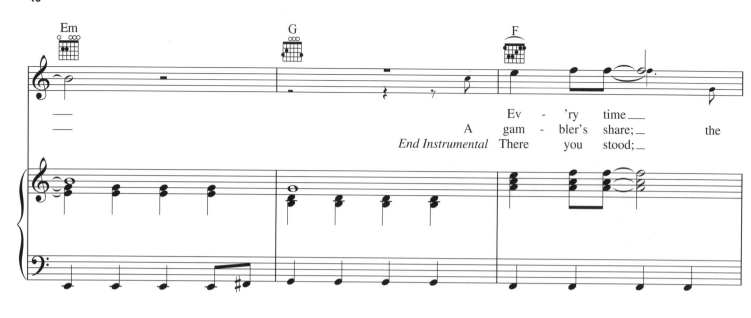

MAINSTREET

Words and Music by
BOB SEGER

43

Copyright © 1976, 1977 Gear Publishing Co.
All Rights Reserved Used by Permission

OLD TIME ROCK & ROLL

Words and Music by GEORGE JACKSON
and THOMAS E. JONES III

Moderate Rock 'n' Roll beat

WE'VE GOT TONIGHT

Words and Music by
BOB SEGER

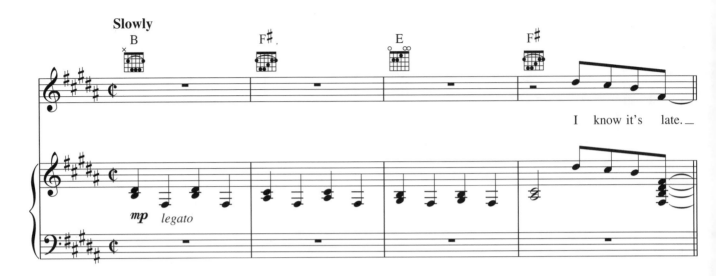

I know it's late.

I know you're wea — ry.   I know your plans __
I've been so lone — ly.   All of my hopes __

don't in - clude me.   Still, here we are,
fad - ing a — way.   I've longed for love __

AGAINST THE WIND

Words and Music by
BOB SEGER

noth - in' left___ to burn___ and noth - in' left to prove.___
wor - ried a - bout pay - in', or e - ven how much I owed.___

End Instrumental

And I re - mem - ber what she___ said to
Mov - in' eight miles a min - ute for months at a
Well, those drift - er's days are___ past me

me,___ how she swore___ that it nev - er would end.___
time,___ break - in' all___ of the rules___ that would bend,___
now.___ I've got so___ much more to___ think a - bout:___

THE FIRE INSIDE

Words and Music by
BOB SEGER

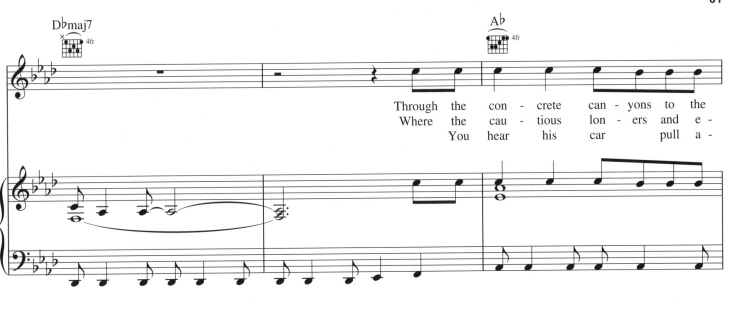

Through the con - crete can - yons to the
Where the cau - tious lon - ers and e -
You hear his car pull a -

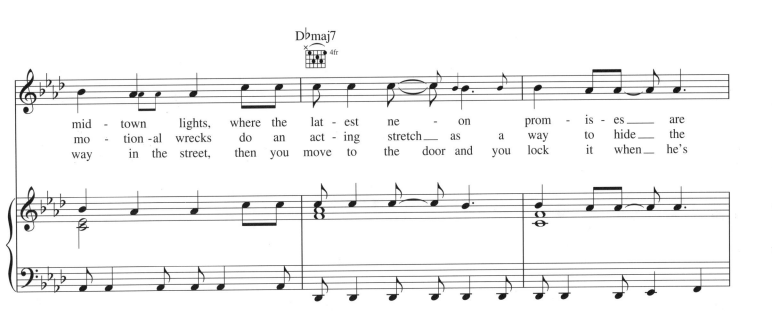

mid - town lights, where the lat - est ne - on prom - is - es ___ are
mo - tion -al wrecks do an act - ing stretch ___ as a way to hide ___ the
way in the street, then you move to the door and you lock it when ___ he's

burn - ing bright. ___
ob - vi - ous. ___
gone for good. ___

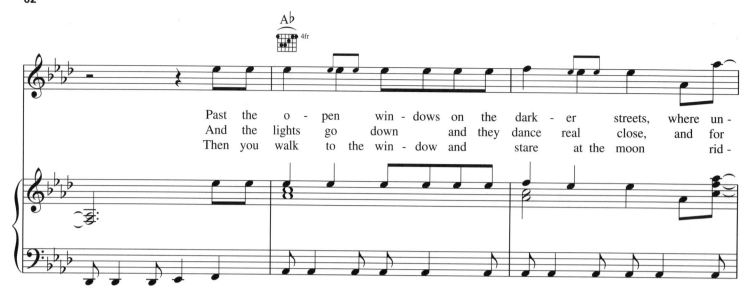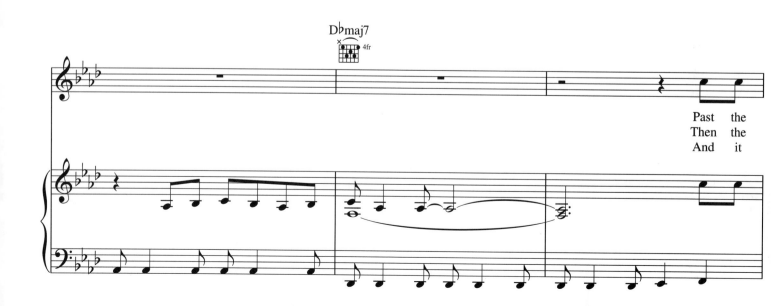

phon - y pos - ers with their worn - out lines, the tired new mon - ey dressed
beat gets loud - er and the mood is gone, the dark - ness scat - ters as the
comes to you how it all slips a - way, youth and beau - ty are

to the nines, ___ the low - life deal - ers with their bad de - signs and the
lights flash on. ___ They hold one an - oth - er just a lit - tle too long and they
gone one day. ___ No mat - ter what you dream or feel or say, it

dil - et - tantes ___ with their o - pen minds. You're out on the town,
move a - part ___ and then move on. On to the street,
ends in dust ___ and dis - ar - ray. Like wind on the plains,

LIKE A ROCK

Words and Music by
BOB SEGER

Additional Lyrics

4. Twenty years now;
   Where'd they go?
   Twenty years;
   I don't know.
   I sit and I wonder sometimes
   Where they've gone.

5. And sometimes late at night,
   When I'm bathed in the firelight,
   The moon comes callin' a ghostly white,
   And I recall.

C'EST LA VIE
(You Never Can Tell)

Words and Music by
CHUCK BERRY

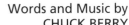

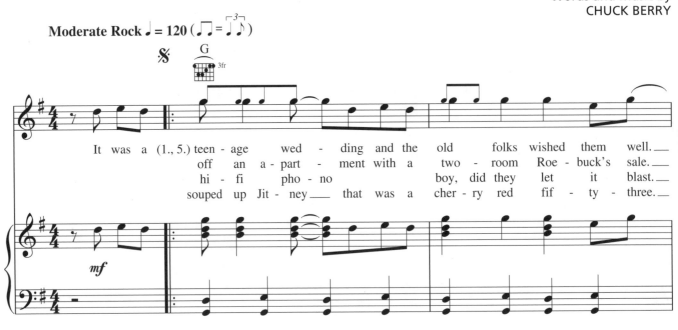

It was a (1., 5.) teen - age wed - ding and the old folks wished them well.
off an a - part - ment with a two - room Roe - buck's sale.
hi - fi pho - no boy, did they let it blast.
souped up Jit - ney that was a cher - ry red fif - ty - three.

You could see that Pi - erre did tru -
The cool - er - a - tor was jammed with T. V.
Sev - en hun - dred lit - tle re - cords all
They drove it down to New Or - leans, cel - e -

- ly love the ma - de - moi - selle.
din - ners and gin - ger ale.
Blues, Rock, Rhy - thm and Jazz.
brate their an - ni - ver - sa - ry.

And now the
And when Pi -
But when the
It was

IN YOUR TIME

Words and Music by
BOB SEGER

the cor - ri - dors____ and riv - er - beds. There'll be
will tum - ble through__ your sum - mer days, by de -
a - cross the great____ un - bro - ken void. All be -

Last Time To Coda ⊕ 1, 3

sign in your_____ time. Tow'r - ing
sign in your_____ *End solo*
nign in your_____ Af - ter

2

time. Feel the wind and set your - self_ the bold -